Finding Out About

CONSERVATION

John Bentley and Bill Charlton

Batsford Academic and Educational Ltd *London*

CONTENTS

Typeset by Tek-Art Ltd, London
and printed in Great Britain by
R.J. Acford
Chichester, Sussex
for the publishers
Batsford Academic and Educational Ltd,
an imprint of B.T. Batsford Ltd,
4 Fitzhardinge Street
London W1H 0AH

ISBN 0 7134 4287 5

Acknowledgments

All photographs and maps in the book were
taken or drawn by the authors, except for the
map on page 21 (London Borough of Bromley
Planning Department) and the map on page
24 (The Ordnance Survey).

The pictures on the front cover show: (top)
the Bingley Five-Rise on the Leeds & Liver-
pool Canal (the authors); (bottom left) the
Market House, Winster, Derbyshire (A.F.
Kersting).

Conservation is an extremely broad topic and if you were to ask a group of people what they understand it to mean, you would very likely get a lot of different answers. Conservation means different things to different people. To some it is mainly about preserving old buildings; others see it as the need to prevent pollution. Some conservation groups, like the many footpath groups, are involved only in local activities; others, like Greenpeace, are international organizations which make newspaper headlines across the world by their attempts to prevent pollution. However, although the particular interests of the various conservation groups vary considerably, there is something they all share in common. This common link is their concern about the quality of the environment — a wish to prevent those parts of the environment which they love and cherish from being damaged or destroyed. That is basically what conservation is about, and what this book is about.

The very fact that so many conservation groups exist shows that there is a need to be concerned about environmental damage. However, thanks to the growing strength of this "conservation movement", many improvements have taken place. In Britain there have been a number of Acts of Parliament which have introduced better ways of protecting and managing our national environment. The Clean Air Acts, for example, have resulted in a reduction in air pollution, and the National Parks and Access to the Countryside Act brought into existence our National Parks. As a result of this legislation, many aspects of conservation work are now the responsibility of civil servants and local government officials, like planning officers and environmental health inspectors. This does not mean that individual people can forget about environmental problems or assume that they are

being satisfactorily dealt with. The officials need the support and interest of the general public if they are to do their jobs effectively, and people can best support conservation when they understand the problems involved.

One of the main ideas suggested by this book is that conservation is important not just in special places like National Parks but everywhere. You ought to be able to find out about most aspects of conservation by studying your own home area, and the book will ask you to go out and look.

You will discover that conservation matters frequently involve conflicts. Conflicts may arise when the interests of one group of people clash with those of another group — for example, when the smell from a factory causes a nuisance to local residents, or when people object to the route of a motorway because it means destroying an area of woodland. When conflicts of interest like this have

to be resolved, there is often no "right" or "wrong" answer. The attitudes people take depend on their points of view and on what their priorities are.

When you come to carry out some of the activities suggested for finding out about conservation in your area, you will find that you come face to face with some of these conflicts. You will discover that conservation problems involve many aspects of life, and you will have to work out what your own priorities are. In particular, you will need to decide how much importance you believe should be placed on the need for conservation, and how far you would be prepared to adjust your own behaviour and personal desires in order to support conservation policies.

You will find that the book is biased. It is in favour of conservation, and we make no apology for this, because we believe that the environment needs the support of ordinary people if it is to survive the pressures which damage it. We hope that you will come to share this point of view too.

The essential source of information is your own local environment. Go out and get to know it. Make maps, take photographs, make notes and, as you observe how things are changing, you will understand the purpose of conservation.

1. ORDNANCE SURVEY MAPS

The Ordnance Survey provides an excellent range of plans and topographic maps, and it is important for the work in this book that you obtain large-scale maps of your local area. The maps required are:

(i) 1 : 1,250 (80 cm to 1 km or approx 50" to 1 mile)
1 : 2,500 (40 cm to 1 km or approx 25" to 1 mile)

These are the largest scales available and, although you will need more than one sheet to cover your local area, these plans will give considerable detail.

(ii) 1 : 10,000 (10 cm to 1 km or approx 6" to 1 mile)
1 : 25,000 (4 cm to 1 km or approx 2½" to 1 mile)
1 : 50,000 (2 cm to 1 km or approx 1" to 1 mile)

With these smaller scales, less detail is shown, but the area covered is larger and these maps are best used for land use studies and for the location of places of interest like National Trust properties or conservation areas.

Remember that, as maps become out-dated, their value does not diminish. The older maps become historical records and show clearly the changes in the local environment.

Information and details about Ordnance Survey maps are available free of charge from the Director General, The Ordnance Survey, Romsey Road, Maybush, Southampton SO9 4DH.

2. GOVERNMENT DEPARTMENTS

(i) *Department of the Environment*, 2, Marsham Street, London SW1P 3EB.
There are also regional offices in Birmingham, Leeds, Manchester, Newcastle, Bristol, Nottingham, N. Ireland. Also, the Education Service of the Directorate of Ancient Monuments and Historic Buildings, 25, Savile Row, London W1X 2BT.

(ii) *Department of Energy,* Thames House South, Millbank, London SW1P 4QJ.
There are also regional conservation offices.

(iii) *Department of Transport*, 2 Marsham Street, London SW1P 3EB.

(iv) *Department of Education and Science,* Elizabeth House, York Road, London SE1 7PH.

3. LOCAL COUNCIL OFFICES

The various departments within a local authority can provide useful information about conservation and planning. The most useful department to approach initially is the Planning Department, where large-scale plans and planning proposals can be consulted.

4. LOCAL LIBRARIES AND MUSEUMS

Libraries have a wide range of useful materials and you should ask a Librarian for guidance. Local libraries will have large-scale maps of different dates which will enable you to trace changes in the land use and buildings of your neighbourhood. Similarly, museums will provide valuable records and information about local and natural history. Ask the Keeper or the Conservator of the museum for guidance on your museum project. Your teacher may be able to arrange for the museum staff to talk to you about the work of the museum and their tasks of conservation.

5. CONSERVATION AND AMENITY GROUPS

There are many societies which you can consult and this is just a selection of some of the best:

Civic Trust, 17, Carlton House Terrace, London SW1Y 5AW.
Council for Environmental Conservation (CPRE), Zoological Gardens, Regents Park, London NW1 4RY.
Council for the Protection of Rural England, 4, Hobart Place, London SW1W 0HY.
Countryside Commission, John Dower House, Crescent Place, Cheltenham, Glos. GL50 3RA.
Forestry Commission, 231, Corstorphine Road, Edinburgh EH12 7AT.
Friends of the Earth, 9, Poland Street, London W1V 3DG.
National Trust, 42, Queen Anne's Gate, London SW1H 9AS.
Nature Conservancy Council (N.C.C.), 19-20, Belgrave Square, London SW1X 8BY.
Ramblers' Association, 1-5, Wandsworth Road, London SW8 2LJ.
Royal Society for the Protection of Birds (R.S.P.B.), The Lodge, Sandy, Beds. SG19 2DL.
Town and Country Planning Association, 17, Carlton House Terrace, London SW1Y 5AS.
"WATCH", c/o Society for the Promotion of Nature Conservation (S.P.N.C.), 22, The Green, Nettleham, Lincoln LN2 2NR.
World Wildlife Fund, 29, Greville Street, London EC1N 8AX.

6. NEWSPAPERS, RADIO AND TELEVISION BROADCASTS

National and local newspapers are essential reading. You should keep a cuttings file or make a display board for "Conservation News Cuttings". Radio and television have many good programmes on conservation topics. B.B.C. Radio 4's regular features include *Wildlife, The Living World* and *Groundswell*.

Conservation in the Local Area

The two photographs here show very different landscapes. One is a Devon village, set in a rural environment, and the other is part of the urban scene of inner London. Both landscapes show signs of change in their new buildings, but, whereas the village has grown slowly over the years, with gradual addition of bungalows and houses, the urban landscape has been virtually rebuilt in recent times. The photographs show two extremes of environmental

◁ *This is the village of Ashprington, Devon. The church tower dates from about 1350. How can you distinguish between the old and the new in this village?*

Amenity Features of a suburban area, listed in the key to a map. This shows some of the environmental features seen as important by a local planning department and which will be kept in mind when plans are made for development in the area. You could use this list to help you plan your Conservation Trail. ▷

◁ *Since the 1950s large parts of South London have been rebuilt. Can you see any signs of the past or opportunities for wildlife in this picture?*

change and illustrate the theme of conservation. Whilst the village has been able to keep the old alongside the new, the urban area has lost most of its past. It is a man-made environment which has replaced almost entirely the natural world.

Landscape change is inevitable and necessary if we are to improve living standards, but how far should we go in making changes? Are some parts worth keeping or is the new always better than the old? Can we afford the expensive waste of materials when houses are pulled down, and what about the loss of features which are irreplaceable, like historic buildings?

These are the sorts of questions asked in conservation, and they apply to important things besides buildings. The main concerns of conservation are wildlife, heritage, amenity and raw materials and these can all be studied in your local area. As the neighbourhood changes, what happens to the world of living things, the animals and plants? Does the variety increase or decrease? What effects do changes have upon the local history? When old workshops or streets are demolished, are valuable parts of your area's heritage being destroyed? Then there is the amenity of a region or a neighbourhood — i.e. the benefit provided by places like parks and open spaces where you can play, or areas which have interesting buildings or attractive scenery. Are the local amenities being maintained or spoilt in the face of change? Finally, there is the concern for resources, particularly the conservation of materials like metals and fossil fuels which, once used, cannot be replaced. What happens to old iron and waste-paper in your area? Does your school conserve energy by insulating the buildings to prevent loss of heat? These questions require us to think carefully and to explore our feelings about the environment and they introduce at the local level problems of conservation which face the whole world.

To help you explore the problems of conservation in your own locality, get each of your friends to make a list of what they think are the 5 most attractive and 5 most unattractive places or buildings in the neighbourhood. Compare and discuss your results and decide, for example, which buildings should be preserved and which should be replaced. With the aid of a large-scale map (O.S. 1:2,500), plan a route or "Conservation Trail" around your school and produce a display of the places that were discussed. Write a report on the signs of change and decide whether you think they are good or bad.

AMENITY FEATURES

REFERENCE

Designated Conservation Areas . . .	▥
Tree Preservation Orders – Areas . .	▦
Single Trees .	●
Tree-lined Roads	○○○ ○○○
Tree cover over roads	◆ ◆ ◆
Hedges and massed vegetation . . .	****
Listed Buildings.	▲
Large important buildings	⌐_
Churches	†
Long range vistas	◁—
Views	▲—
Boundary of area	▬

Conservation Costs Money

One constant feature of the environment is that it is always changing. Nothing stays the same, and conservation is, therefore, a difficult and expensive business. Changes created by man and machine can be stopped if really necessary, but changes caused by the natural processes of weathering and erosion and the slow evolution of planet Earth cannot be stopped. The best we can do is to slow down those natural processes of change and decay by careful maintenance and repair.

The costs involved in conservation are apparent in every neighbourhood, and the money is not only spent on things of special significance. Every year, local authorities spend millions of pounds repairing roads and water mains damaged by winter frosts, and, in the summer, their problem is to cut back the trees and weeds which overgrow the roads and footpaths. Schools, too, must be repainted periodically, including the white lines of the games pitches in the playground. Even the conservation of wildlife habitats requires expenditure, to stop the natural processes of change. For example, if the Norfolk Broads were not carefully managed but left to nature, the lakes would silt up and the present habitats, on which rare species of plants and insects depend, would soon disappear.

It requires continued expenditure of time and money to maintain our gardens and wildlife refuges and to protect our streets and houses, and, of course, the older the properties, the more expensive it becomes. The conservation of a sixteenth-century thatched cottage, which was once the home of a distinguished person, may be important, but someone has to be prepared to pay those extra costs. Repairs will be needed more frequently and require special materials which are in keeping with the style and age of the building. It would spoil the appearance of the cottage to give it a new roof of concrete tiles.

Besides the costs of general maintenance, conservation also costs money when we decide not to develop an area or adopt modern methods of production. The conservation of a historic town centre preserves an attractive environment, but it means that the

Without regular repainting the woodwork would begin to rot and need to be replaced before long. If a house has to be repainted approximately every 7 years, how many times could this building have been redecorated? It was built in 1897. ▷

traffic becomes congested in the narrow streets and it costs far more in time and money for shops and customers to carry on business. A farmer may decide not to drain the marshland on his farm because of its value to wildlife. As a result, the land is more difficult to use and the farming is less efficient and more expensive.

The photographs show two examples of everyday conservation. How much does it cost to repaint a house or put a new roof on a building? Make a survey of your home or school buildings and, on an annotated sketch drawing or plan, indicate where repairs are needed. See if you can get hold of a house surveyor's report to give you some idea about the sort of things you should be looking for. Finally, make a survey in the area of your school and list all the different types of conservation work that are in progress — things such as hedge-trimming, road and pavement repairs.

These old buildings in Durham have been neglected for many years and now need expensive repairs. It may be cheaper to use modern materials but would they be appropriate?

Wasted and Unused Land

In a small and densely peopled country like Britain, one of the most important of all our resources is our land. We use land for an enormous number of purposes — the list is almost endless. Go through the alphabet from A to Z, starting with "agriculture" and ending with "zoo", and see if you can find a land-use to fit every letter.

There are some things for which more land is needed every year — new roads and new houses, for example — but, since the total amount of land in the country is fixed, we can only find the land for these new developments if we give up something else. In Britain, what we are giving up most of all is our farmland. Look around you, at the edge of any town, and you will see how urban growth is nibbling away at the countryside, and converting fields into buildings.

The pity is that we do not need to lose nearly so much of our precious countryside in this way, because there is an enormous quantity of other land which is lying idle and is therefore being wasted. According to the Department of the Environment, there were 43,000 hectares of derelict land in England alone, when the last survey of derelict land was made in 1974. Much of this is land so

This small plot of waste land is only 100 metres from a busy high street. Are there any places like this close to your home?

severely damaged by past industrial use that it would take a lot of money to reclaim it. However, there is possibly two or three times as much as this, just lying unused and neglected, most of which could easily be used for new developments. Most of this wasted land is in our cities, and much of it is owned by the local authorities and other official bodies.

It is important that we should know how much land is being wasted like this, and where it is, so that we can try to find new uses for it. In this way, we might be able to prevent the

This area of old housing is being cleared by the local council, but, unless they have the money, it will lie idle for many years. Why have they fenced the area?

loss of more countryside. Try to find out how much derelict, unused or even just neglected land there is in your own neighbourhood. You can begin by making a survey on a large-scale map — an Ordnance Survey, 1:2,500 would be best, but a good street map will do. Examine your area street by street and shade in on the map any examples of wasted land you can find, however small. Mark each example with a number, to identify it, and write a short description of each one, giving your suggestions for improvement or re-use. If you want to find out more about the history of any of your wasted areas, you should be able to get information from the planning office, or from local amenity groups.

Refurbishment and Urban Renewal

What are the advantages of refurbishing these houses rather than building new ones?

A typical family house is generally expected to last for about 75 years, assuming that it is maintained properly and pipes are mended and the woodwork is repainted when required. Eventually, these minor repairs will not keep pace with the general decay of the brickwork and plaster, and either expensive major repairs are necessary or the house has to be replaced. But houses do not just wear out; they also become old-fashioned. Old houses do not provide the facilities that are expected nowadays, like hot and cold running water, a proper bathroom and an indoor lavatory.

In Britain, during the nineteenth century, our towns and cities grew very rapidly as centres of industry. Many houses were built quickly, to accommodate the industrial workers. By the mid-twentieth century these same houses had gone beyond or were close to the end of their useful lives. There has been an urgent need to replace or modernize such dwellings. It is a problem which is found in the inner areas of all our major industrial cities. Many of these areas became "slums", and, in the period since the Second World War, extensive inner-city districts have been rebuilt.

In the 1950s and 1960s the popular solution was to make a complete redevelopment of these areas. The grid-iron street patterns of terraced houses were bull-dozed away and these were replaced by tower blocks of flats. By building upwards, more open space was made available for cars and recreation. It was a planner's dream of the carefully organized urban landscape. It seemed like a good idea at the time, but people who were rehoused found many drawbacks in these redevelop-

renovate their dwellings. The advantages for conservation are obvious, for not only are materials conserved but the character of urban neighbourhoods is preserved.

What policies of urban renewal have been used in your locality? You may not find extensive areas of change, but look for individual houses or streets where removal or refurbishment has taken place. Contact the planning department of your local authority and find out what grants are available for the modernization of houses. Make a map of your local area and mark on it those areas where urban renewal, refurbished homes or new housing can be found. Write a report to accompany your map and say whether or not the environment has been improved, in your opinion.

This redevelopment scheme of high-rise flats and new open spaces has replaced streets of old houses. What advantages and disadvantages can you think of, arising out of this change?

ments. The tower blocks destroyed any sense of community, and people felt lonely and isolated, trapped, up in the air. The policy of urban redevelopment was also very expensive and wasteful of building materials.

As a result of the social problems and the wasteful expense, there has been, during the 1970s, a marked change in the policy of urban renewal. The move has been towards a policy of conservation, of "mend and make-do". Where possible, old houses are refurbished, instead of being pulled down. The houses are repaired and modernized. The government has made grants available, to help local authorities and private home-owners

This map shows a pattern of housing renewal and modernization in a suburban neighbourhood. This should now be compared with Ordnance Survey maps of the area or with a map showing the age of buildings, in order to explain some of the changes.

13

Listed Buildings

Look at the buildings in any of our old towns and you cannot fail to notice the rich variety of architectural styles. Styles of building are often associated with particular historical periods, and they help us to understand more about living in the past. Sometimes a particular building is especially important because of an incident which happened there or, perhaps, because it was the home of a famous person. These buildings are part of our national heritage. We try to keep them in good condition and prevent them from deteriorating.

Ever since 1953 the government has been keeping lists of buildings of special architectural or historic interest. Any building which appears on these lists is called a "listed building", and this is an indication of its importance. All buildings built before 1700 are listed, provided that they have survived in anything like their original condition. For the period after 1700 we have a great many buildings, and only a selection of those built between 1700 and 1914 are listed. A start has been made on listing a selection of buildings from the 1914-1939 period.

When the experts consider whether or not to "list" a building, they pay particular attention to a number of factors — special architectural value, illustration of social or economic history (e.g. schools, markets, prisons), special

"Dove Cottage", Grasmere, is a Grade I listed building because it used to be the home of the poet William Wordsworth. In which National Park is this?

techniques (cast iron or concrete), association with well-known characters or events, examples of town planning. The importance of a building is shown by its grading. Grade I buildings are of exceptional interest, and only about 4 per cent are in this category. Grades II and III indicate lesser importance.

We already have more than a quarter of a million listed buildings. Just because a building is listed does not mean that it will be preserved in all circumstances, but it does mean that it cannot be demolished without official permission and that any alterations must preserve its character as far as possible. Owners of listed buildings can sometimes get grants or loans to help with repairs and maintenance.

You can find out more about the listed buildings in your area from the planning department of your local authority. Each local authority area keeps details of gradings, together with descriptive notes on all listed buildings within its boundaries. In some places the list may run to thousands of buildings.

Make a selection of listed buildings constructed at different dates and find out from your library what styles of building were popular at those times. Go and look at the buildings themselves and see if you can identify those features which make them important. If you come across a building associated with a famous person, see if you can find out more about what the association was with your town.

This terrace of early-nineteenth-century houses is listed Grade II because of its architectural merits. What are the distinctive features?

Conservation Societies

The British people have long been one of the leading supporters of conservation movements, both in our own country and in the world at large. The government supports the conservation of historic buildings, beautiful landscapes, wildlife and new material resources through the Department of the Environment. This department is particularly concerned with matters of planning, land use and environmental protection, but all government departments have a responsibility to keep in mind the desirability of conserving our national heritage.

Most of the laws designed to promote conservation are carried out through the authority of local councils, who are responsible for the planning in their own areas, including such varied things as urban renewal, green belts and tree preservation.

Besides these authorities, the important government body responsible for conservation and the environment is the Countryside Commission. One of its major responsibilities is the organization of the National Parks (see page 30.) If you write to the Countryside Commission you can find out more about its work.

The strength of government support for conservation reflects the wide concern and active interest shown by the many private and voluntary societies which flourish in Britain. Even in the middle of the nineteenth century, private individuals were actively pressing for conservation. The rising tide of industry was seen as a threat to the historic buildings and countryside. In 1865, John Stuart Mill and T.H. Huxley were among those who established the Commons, Open Spaces and Footpaths Preservation Society. In 1877, a society for the protection of ancient buildings was founded.

Today, the largest private conservation society is the National Trust. Its full title is the National Trust for Places of Historic

Bodiam Castle in East Sussex was built in the fourteenth century as a defence against a threatened invasion from France. It is typical of the kind of buildings maintained by the National Trust.
▽

You will see this symbol wherever you come across property owned by the National Trust. Are there any National Trust properties in your area?

Interest and Natural Beauty. It was established as an independent organization in 1895 and today owns over 240 buildings, 180,000 hectares of land and 400 miles of coastline. It is the largest private landowner in the country. The two main objectives are (i) the conservation of beautiful buildings and landscapes and (ii) the provision of access to these places for the public. One of its important projects was Enterprise Neptune, a scheme to purchase and preserve areas of unspoilt coastal scenery. It started in 1965 and the National Trust now has saved from development about 400 miles of coastline.

The Civic Trust is another leading voluntary society concerned with conservation. It was founded in 1957, with the purpose of improving the appearance of town and country environments. It acts as a central organization for the many local conservation trusts, and it organizes educational projects for schools.

The Civic Trust is very active in urban areas, campaigning for preservation of historic buildings and even sponsoring the conservation of a complete town in Derbyshire, the small settlement of Wirksworth.

Are there any areas of your neighbourhood which need improvement? Find out the sort of schemes that are organized by the Civic Trust (your local library will be able to help you) and you can then produce your own environmental study. Find out, too, what conservation societies exist in your area and make a display to show the range of their activities. If there is a part of the environment which is not cared for, perhaps you should set about organizing your own society.

Museums

Museums are traditional, well-established ways of preserving things from the past. They are places of safe-keeping where objects, often of extreme rarity and value, are displayed. The objects can range from antiquities of ancient Egypt to the stuffed bodies of extinct animals. As well as being places of exhibition, most museums act as centres of research and restoration, helping us to understand how the world and its civilizations have developed.

The main growth of museums in Britain was during the Victorian period, and all our major cities have museums, often housed in large ornate buildings close to the city centre. Museums generally grew from private collections of antiquities which had been presented to the nation or to city councils. The world's largest museum, the British Museum, began in this way. During the late eighteenth century several wealthy persons bequeathed their family treasure to the nation, and, to provide a home for these valuables, the British Museum was built, and completed by 1847. Apart from the books, the museum is said to contain more than 8 million items, including such unique exhibits as the Magna Carta, which was agreed by King John in 1215. Other national collections and exhibitions soon followed and, by the beginning of the twentieth century, South Kensington was the "museum area" of London, with the Natural

This is a traditional local museum. What type of things would you expect to find in a place like this?

History Museum, the Geological Museum, the Science Museum and the Victoria and Albert Museum.

Small local museums have generally displayed a wide range of items, including works of art, geological specimens and domestic utensils. However, many of the newer museums concentrate on particular themes. In London, for example, there is the London Transport Museum at Covent Garden and, alongside the River Thames, you can either visit the National Maritime Museum at Greenwich or explore actual ships, like the *Cutty Sark* or *H.M.S. Belfast*, which are preserved as museum pieces.

Museums used to be seen as rather dull places, with large, silent rooms in which you would find glass cabinets filled with labelled objects. Today, museums use many different ways of explaining and displaying the past. The Gladstone Pottery Museum in Longton, Stoke-on-Trent, is housed in a restored potbank. This is one of many modern museums where you can see things being made in the way they used to be. There are also open-air museums where not one but several former ways of life are displayed in realistic settings. At Beamish, in County Durham, there is the North of England Open Air Museum and there you can walk around reconstructed buildings and working machines from the region's industrial past.

Why don't you make your own local museum? See how well you can display "treasures" of the local history that appeal to you. You can make copies and working models of the real things, just as many museums do, and then write a short description about your own museum piece. If you can, visit a museum in your area, to get some ideas and guidance about the ways museums restore and display the treasures in their care.

This is the clipper, Cutty Sark, preserved as a museum beside the River Thames in Greenwich. What are the advantages of this kind of preservation?

Conservation Areas in Towns

Have you ever felt disappointed or sad when a building you particularly liked has been knocked down to make way for something new? If you live in a town, you might have had this feeling quite often, because our towns have changed a lot in recent years, as a result of what we call "redevelopment".

Any buildings which come under the heading of "listed buildings" (see pages 14-15) are protected against demolition and change, but there are many attractive buildings or groups of buildings which do not have this official protection, and which it would be a shame to lose. It might be a cluster of houses and shops beside an old green, marking the position of a former village centre; or a street of houses and corner shops which are typical of the kind of building which was widespread at the end of the nineteenth century. If there were no restrictions on development, we might lose areas like these — and once they have gone, they are lost for ever. Can you think of any favourite areas in your neighbourhood?

One of the jobs that local authority planning departments have to do is to advise their councils about redevelopment schemes, and help them to decide whether to give their approval or not. In 1967 the government passed an Act of Parliament (called the Civic Amenities Act) which encouraged the councils to define special areas as "conservation areas". These conservation areas are often quite small, perhaps no more than a street or two, and the idea behind the scheme is to try to preserve the particular character of that area. When applications are put forward for any kind of development inside a conservation area, the council will want to examine the plans very carefully before giving their consent.

You can find out from your own planning department whether there are any conservation areas in your locality. You might be able to go to have a look at one of them, and perhaps take some photographs of the kind of view which makes it special. The photographs can be mounted on a piece of card, with a paragraph of description beside them, under the heading "Conservation Area".

Perhaps there is a particular corner of your neighbourhood which you and your friends would like to protect from changes. You could make your own suggestions for a conservation area. You would have to draw a very careful map (say, on a scale of 1:2,500), showing the boundary of the proposed area, together with the details of the features you want to preserve — buildings, trees, footpaths, etc. You could take photographs of these features and use them to illustrate a written description in which you justify your choice. If it is well done, you could even submit it to the council!

This is part of the conservation area in Canterbury. ▷ What reasons can you see for preserving it in its present form?

BOUNDARY OF CONSERVATION AREA . . . . . . ___ ___

BUILDINGS WHICH DO NOT CONTRIBUTE TO THE CHARACTER OF THE AREA . . . . . .

BUILDINGS WHICH MAKE AN IMPORTANT CONTRIBUTION TO THE CHARACTER OF THE AREA . . . .

BUILDINGS ESSENTIAL TO THE CHARACTER OF THE AREA . . . .

TREE GROUP ESSENTIAL TO THE CHARACTER OF THE AREA . . . .

INDIVIDUAL TREES ESSENTIAL TO THE CHARÁCTER OF THE AREA . . . .

EYESORE – UNTIDY SPOT IN NEED OF ATTENTION. . . . .

INTERESTING STREET-LIGHT FITTINGS . . . . . .

IMPORTANT VIEWS. . . . .

This row of houses in South London is not part of an official conservation area, but is a "general improvement area" and the houses receive grants for repairs and modernization. It is another form of conservation. Do you feel that the parked cars create a nuisance?

This is part of a map of a conservation area prepared by the Planning Department of the London Borough of Bromley. Use the headings in the key to help you define a conservation area in your neighbourhood.

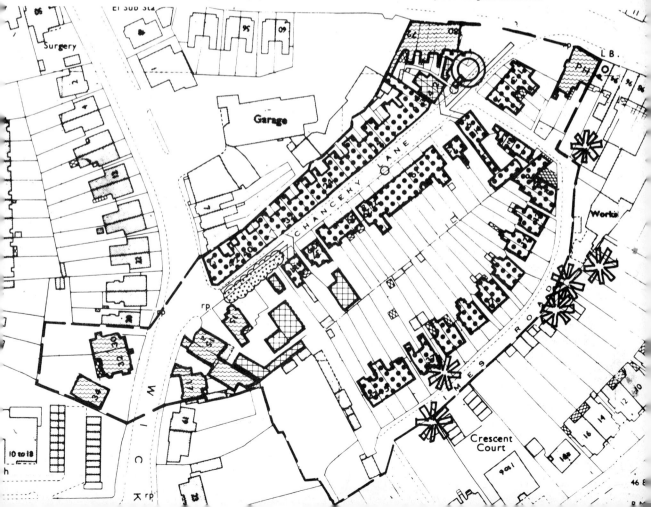

Trees in the Landscape

There is a tree preservation order on this clump of trees because without them the neighbourhood would be much less attractive.

Trees have a special place in British landscapes and we are fortunate to have such a large variety of trees to enjoy. We sometimes take our trees for granted, and it takes a tragic happening, like the outbreak of Dutch Elm Disease in the 1970s (which killed most of the elms in southern England), to make us appreciate what we have lost.

Trees used to be found over a much greater area of Britain than they are today. When the Romans came, 2,000 years ago, most of the country was forested. Since that time most of the forested areas have gradually been cleared, either to make space for farmland, or to provide wood for fuel or timber for building. Nowadays, we still have lots of uses for timber and wood products like pulp and cellu-

lose — not to mention the fruit we get from orchards.

Trees, like farm crops, are "renewable" resources, and woodland has a high commercial value. For this reason, we are now re-planting trees on land which is too poor for farming. The government organization which is mainly responsible for this "re-afforestation" policy is the Forestry Commission.

The pleasure and enjoyment we get from having trees to look at in the landscape are part of what we call our "amenity". The amenity of an area is made up of those things which make it pleasant or attractive. Many of you will have your own favourite trees which you perhaps see from a window or pass on a

The woodland at the far side of the field is an ▷ attractive feature of the landscape and an important refuge for wildlife. What should happen if the farmer wants to clear it to grow more crops?

regular walk, and which you would really miss if they were not there. Trees are often especially precious to townspeople, because they bring nature into the man-made environment and provide beauty throughout the changing seasons, often in parks. Sometimes a group of trees — or a single tree, even — can be seen to be particularly important to the amenity of a neighbourhood. In such cases, people can apply to their local authority for a tree preservation order, to prevent the trees being felled without official permission.

Remember that it can take many decades for some trees to grow to maturity. We have previous generations to thank for today's trees and, in the same way, we ourselves have a responsibility to future generations to plant new trees for people to enjoy in fifty or even a hundred years from now.

Write to the Parks Department of your local council and find out what policy they have regarding the care of trees in your area.

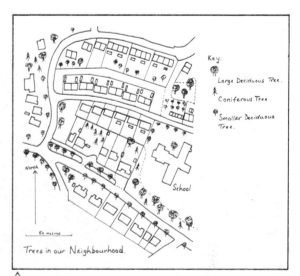

Even in inner city areas you will find a considerable number of trees. Make a survey of the trees in your neighbourhood on a large-scale map. A next step could be to identify with a colour code the different types of tree shown and to note how each tree affects its surroundings through the year.

Green Belts

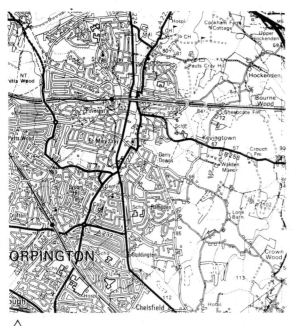

This extract from the O.S. map Sheet 177 (1:50,000) shows clearly the boundary between the built-up area and the open countryside of the Green Belt on the south-eastern edge of London.

This wooded golf course is less than 10 miles from central London, preserved as part of the Green Belt. How can we justify not using this land for housing or industry?

Most people in Britain live in towns, and, although there are parks, playing fields and other open spaces where it is possible to get away from the busy streets and the buildings, a trip into the countryside has a special attraction.

During the period between the First and the Second World Wars, the towns and cities in Britain began to grow outwards very quickly. This was especially true in Southeast England, where houses and factories filled in the gaps between London itself and the ring of small towns about 10 miles away. People became worried that London would keep on growing, swallowing up more and more countryside, so that eventually there would be no rural areas left close enough to the city — nowhere where people could enjoy being among fields and woodlands.

This concern became so strong that, in 1938, a "Green Belt" was set up by Act of Parliament. The Green Belt is a belt of land encircling London from about 10-25 miles out, in which the agricultural character of the landscape is to be preserved. Since then green belts have been set up around other large cities. Even in places where there is no official

green belt, the local authorities are concerned to try to preserve the rural nature of the nearby countryside.

In order for people to be able to enjoy visiting the countryside, there has to be a good network of roads and footpaths, to provide access. Most of the land is private property, containing valuable crops or animals, and, without good footpaths, much beautiful countryside is inaccessible to the public.

Unfortunately, over the years, the situation in many places has deteriorated. The rural landscapes have sometimes changed, as farmland has been converted to non-agricultural uses. Many eyesores have been created by the unsociable behaviour of people who vandalize property or tip rubbish. Sometimes footpaths have been lost, because farmers have ploughed them over or blocked entry, or they have become overgrown through neglect. Some places, often near water, have become so popular with visitors that they are being literally eroded away.

Find out how the countryside around your town has been standing up to the pressures of having a town on its doorstep. Contact your local council to see whether there is an official green belt and find out where its boundaries are. Choose a section of countryside up against the built-up area — say, about one square kilometre — and see if you can get a 1:10,000 map of the area. Find out what access roads and footpaths there are and check with the planning department to make sure that the map information is up-to-date. There might be a footpaths group in your area to contact. Use your map to carry out a survey of the area, distinguishing between agricultural and non-agricultural land uses. Use special symbols to indicate eyesores and places where access is not possible or where the land has been worn away by too many visitors.

This housing development is on the outer edge of London's Green Belt. What are the benefits and losses involved in building in rural areas?

Farming and Conservation

Although Britain is a relatively small country, only about half the size of France, our farmers can produce up to 75% of our food requirements. To achieve this, the land has to be farmed intensively, and the British farmer is among the most efficient in the world.

In spite of competition from other land users, like industry and housing, the area of farmland in Britain has remained fairly stable over recent years, but the amount of food produced has generally increased. These increased yields result from the considerable

In what ways do you think the use of these machines has altered the character and life of the countryside?

improvements in farming methods. The improvements are very necessary because farming, like any business, must produce profit.

Unfortunately, some of the most profitable methods of farming produce more food at the expense of our rural landscapes and wildlife. The balance between efficient food production and conservation of the countryside is a difficult one to maintain. Take, for example, the use of machinery which you can see in the photograph on the left. The machines are expensive to buy and to operate, but they can save a lot of money that would have been spent on employing farm labourers. Just one of these machines can do the work of several men, and in a much shorter time. Machines are more profitable, but, to use them effectively, you need large open fields, similar to those you would find on the prairies of Canada. Therefore, the existing pattern of small fields and hedgerows has to be changed. The field boundaries must be pulled up and several small fields are combined to make one large field suitable for the machine.

Since 1945, it is estimated that 140,000 miles of hedgerow have been removed from

What are the advantages to the farmer in removing this hedge? Why is this considered bad for conservation?

the countryside. In some counties the destruction of hedges has been particularly severe. Between 1946 and 1970 Norfolk lost about 8,000 miles of its hedgerows, which is about 50 per cent of the total. With each year that passes it is reckoned that our countryside loses a further 2,000 miles. Rural landscapes which were once an attractive patchwork of fields and different crops are becoming uninterrupted expanses of windswept prairie. Without the hedges as windbreaks, the important topsoil of some farms is being swept away.

The loss of hedgerows means, of course, that there is more land available for production, but, for the conservationist, it means a loss of a wide variety of plants. The use of herbicides and fertilizers also reduces the number of wild plants growing on the farmland. The modern management of grassland means killing off the "weeds", and so wildflowers like green-winged orchid, snakeshead fritillary and meadow saxifrage are disappearing. The fact that we can still see plenty of buttercups and daisies in the fields does not prove that fewer common plants are threatened. Remember, too, that if we destroy plants, we also destroy the creatures that live on them, and so animals and insects are also threatened.

The use of machines, the application of herbicides, the drainage of marshland and the ploughing up of moorland to increase the farm size all mean more productive farming, and food prices are kept lower than they would otherwise be. If we feel it is wrong for the farmer to make these changes, are we prepared to pay more for our food? Have a discussion with your friends on this question, and, to help you gain more information, start a scrapbook of newspaper cuttings about changes in farming and the conflicts with the countryside.

Wildlife

The collection of articles and newspaper cuttings shown here covers a wide variety of wildlife concerns. There is the threat of a new woodland pest, the great spruce bark beetle, which could seriously damage coniferous plantations, and there is the sad news that Britain's butterflies are in serious decline. Natural habitats essential for the survival of wildlife are being destroyed by man's activities, and it is reported that birdwatching can warn us about the stealthy advance of pollution. A happier note is the report that one farmer is managing to combine successful farming and the conservation of wildlife. It is clear that conservation of animals and insects is seen as a priority and that change is rapid and generally for the worse.

Although, in many of the reports, man is seen as the villian, some of the changes in wildlife are the result of purely natural processes, such as the spread of the spruce beetle. Outbreaks of pests and disease, climatic change and volcanic eruptions are just a few of the natural events which can affect wildlife. Under the laws of nature, these wounds will heal as the old habitats are re-established or new ones emerge.

When man causes the damage, it is often the process of healing which is destroyed, as well as the habitat. Man creates change so rapidly that nature cannot readjust, and animals become extinct. Thus, the variety of species is reduced and this further limits recovery.

One reason for the disappearance of wildlife and the destruction of habitats is simply the pressure of too many people. Just look at the limited number of wildlife species in an urban area. The pressure of population is serious in parts of our country, but it is the attitudes and actions of man that can cause more extensive and greater damage. Some

These cuttings from newspapers and magazines reflect the concern for wildlife felt by many people. As you can see, they are not all man-made problems.

species of wildlife have been hunted to extinction in Britain. Farming, in its pursuit of efficiency, requires uniform land quality with no competition from weeds or pests. The result is the clearance and destruction of things that get in the way, like woodland and marshland habitats, birds of prey, bumble bees and badgers.

A further effect of the improvement of farmland and the general spread of housing, roads and industry is the gradual reduction in the size of wildlife refuges. In the south of England, for example, there used to be a belt of heathland from Kent through to Dorset. Now, only fragments remain, and many are too small to sustain a stable wildlife population.

Death in the countryside.
i) Birds, like this magpie, are often killed by cars. Do you think we are doing enough to protect our wildlife?
ii) Dead elm trees stand bare amidst the greenery of a summer landscape. They were not killed by man, but by a fungus carried by a beetle.

The Nature Conservancy Council, created in 1949, is the major government body today which promotes nature conservation through its National Nature Reserves and Sites of Special Scientific Interest. A major voluntary society is the Royal Society for the Protection of Birds, and it has established sanctuaries and reserves which maintain essential habitats for birds and wildlife generally. Write to these organizations and find out more about their work. "Friends of the Earth" is a conservation group with a worldwide membership. See if there is a local branch in your area and read some of their publications. Learn how to identify the different types of birds and butterflies and keep a record of those observed in your local area. Make a study of the open spaces around you, like gardens and the school grounds, and see if there are ways of making them more attractive habitats for wildlife. You may find that your local council has ways in which it tries to encourage wildlife in local parks and on roadside verges.

Outstanding Landscapes

THE NATIONAL PARKS OF ENGLAND AND WALES

This is a typical setting within the Lake District National Park. What do you feel makes this kind of landscape so special?

Although Britain is a relatively small country, we are fortunate in having a considerable variety of scenery. Attractive scenery can be found almost anywhere in Britain, but there are some areas of such exceptional beauty that we think of them as part of our national heritage. We have a responsibility to preserve these landscapes for the future, and so we try to protect them against changes which would spoil their character.

In England and Wales (Scotland is different), the most important of these special areas are the National Parks, of which there are ten — Dartmoor, Exmoor, Pembrokeshire Coast, Brecon Beacons, Snowdonia, Peak District, Lake District, Yorkshire Dales, North York Moors and Northumberland. A number of other landscapes have been designated as Areas of Outstanding Natural Beauty (AONB), and particularly attractive sections of coast have been given the status of Heritage Coasts. In none of these instances does the special designation (National Park, AONB, Heritage Coast) provide complete protection from undesirable changes, though it ensures that government and local authority planners will look very carefully at any proposals for change, in order to assess their possible effect on the landscape.

One of the problems about the conservation of scenery is that much of the land is privately owned. If an individual wishes to exercise his right to develop the resources of his land for his own benefit — say, by clearing a woodland, or building a supermarket — other people may object, perhaps on the grounds that the appearance will be unattractive, or the development might cause noise or smells — i.e. it might cause a "loss of amenity". The conflict of interests which may arise between an individual and the general community over matters of conservation can be a serious problem, and it has to be resolved fairly. How much freedom do you think an individual should have to develop his property in a way which might give offence to other people? Do you think it is fair that, say, farmers who happen to live in National Parks should be less free to change their farming practices (because they might spoil the scenery) than farmers outside the National Parks? How far do you think such problems can be satisfactorily resolved?

If you have the opportunity of visiting a National Park, you can find out how the park authorities carry out their tasks of preserving the landscape and helping visitors. All the parks have information centres and you can obtain addresses of these from your local library. Find out what kinds of activities are organized in the National Park you want to visit. During your stay in the park give some thought to the quality of the scenery. Find a good vantage point and study the view carefully. After you have taken in the overall view, try to identify all the small details which make up the landscape — shape of hills, pattern and colour of fields, trees, rocky outcrops, glimpses of water, buildings, noises, and so on. Make a note of these details and, if you can, draw a sketch as a record, or take a photograph if you prefer. Try to imagine the kind of changes which would spoil that scenery.

This footpath has been repaired because it had been "worn out" by the many visitors. How can we stop the deterioration of beautiful landscapes and, at the same time, make them more accessible to the public?

Local Pressure Groups

When you consult your local newspaper or read the posters and pamphlets in a local library, you will discover that lots of people are "angry" or "concerned" about the changes affecting the character of the local environment. As you can see from this collection of newspaper cuttings, interest generally centres on the built environment. People are protesting against new building developments and changes in land use, or questioning the way in which rate-payers' money is spent.

When several people in a neighbourhood or town share a common concern and wish to make their opinions known, they join together to organize a more effective campaign. The greater publicity which is achieved enables them to create more pressure for their point of view. A typical local pressure group is a residents' association, which will consist of the householders living in a particular street or residential neighbourhood. Their main purpose is to look after the amenities of their neighbourhood; to ensure, for example, that the local council keeps roads and pavements in a good state of repair or that the dustbins are emptied regularly. If there is a planning proposal for new houses or alterations to existing properties, which affects the area, the residents' association will be ensuring that

With their bold headlines, newspapers help us to keep track of the changes in the environment. See if there are similar reports in your local paper.

Lorries can be both a menace and a benefit. Make a list of the good and bad effects that lorries have on the environment. Would you be for or against lorries?

Are there any local conservation groups like this in your area? See if you can find any similar signs.

there would be no loss of environmental quality as a result.

Some pressure groups represent the views which apply to a specific planning development. The building of a new motorway is a subject which always causes considerable controversy and often brings pressure groups representing different opinions into sharp conflict.

Other groups are organized to protect local amenity areas or beauty spots, like the Conservators of Ashdown Forest, or to protest against the problems caused by heavy lorries which thunder through villages and threaten to shake the houses to bits.

Many local pressure groups find that the attitudes they wish to promote are held in common with other groups in the country, and even further pressure can be brought to bear by organizing or joining a national society. The Civic Trust is a society which represents local conservation groups (see page 17), and the Council for the Preservation of Rural England is a national body concerned with the protection of villages and village life.

Your local library or your local council offices will have lists of the local pressure groups, like residents' associations and conservation societies. Find out what they are and what they do. How do they organize their campaigns and publicize their views? Some of them will be prepared to come to talk to you about their work and, perhaps, try to get you to help them achieve their objectives.

Public Participation

The Town and Country Planning Act of 1947 made it a legal requirement that changes in land use or development of property could be carried out only with the permission of a local planning authority. In 1969 a further step was the requirement that all planning procedures must include an opportunity for public discussion before any final decisions are made. This principle of public participation in planning enables local pressure groups or individuals to play their part in the conservation or development of their own areas.

The London Borough of Bromley, as a local authority, is responsible for planning and the implementation of Acts of Parliament. See if you can find out more about the Civic Amenities Act, 1967.

The head of planning is, in theory, the Secretary of State at the Department of the Environment, but the detailed plans for local areas are really the responsibility of two authorities. First, there is the county planning authority, known as the strategic authority, which is responsible for producing a structure plan for the country. This is a planning document of general guidelines. It is then left to the local or district authority to produce the detailed local plans, in conformity with the guidelines of the structure plan.

The local development plan is the document which, with the aid of large-scale maps, charts the ways in which an area's land use, conservation districts, buildings and local roads will develop. With the local plan established, the local authority can initiate action area plans and exercise control over planning applications from private individuals.

An action area plan is a detailed plan for a specific site, like a slum clearance project or the redevelopment of a town centre. In line with the principle of public participation, an action area plan has to have public discussion and a miniumum time of six weeks is allowed for consultation.

An action area plan is produced by the planning department of a local authority, guided by the policies of the local council; but individuals also become involved in planning, whenever they want to make substantial alterations to their own homes or even cut down a tree, if it has a tree preservation order on it. All individual planning applications are submitted to the local planning authority. They are then listed and made available to the public. Those affected by a particular plan, such as a residents' association or adjoining house-owners, are also informed. When the objections and comments of the public have been received, the planning department sub-

What is your opinion of the planning decision which placed this new building in front of the tower of Canterbury Cathedral?

mits them, along with the planning proposal, to the local council, which makes the final decision on whether the development can take place or not. It may seem a complicated and long-drawn-out procedure, but it allows people to take an active interest in the character of their towns.

Contact your local council's planning department and find out the details of the local development plan. What plans does it have for your neighbourhood? Consult the local paper or visit the library and see what planning proposals have been made for your locality. Locate each proposal on a large-scale map (O.S. 1:10,000 or 1:2,500). What effect will they have on the character of the area? Can you detect any areas where change is particularly marked or absent? Why could this be?

Litter and Vandalism

*There are many ways of supporting
the drive to keep Britain tidy. How can you help?*

In several of the pictures in this book, you can find some mention or evidence of litter and vandalism. No matter how much effort is made by the majority to improve and care for the environment, the thoughtless behaviour of a minority can spoil it. The dropping of a drink carton or a plastic bag may seem by itself to be a harmless act, but, if everybody begins to drop their rubbish, the streets and countryside can soon look very messy.

Paper and organic rubbish, like apple-cores, are bio-degradable; that means they will, in time, rot and return to the soil. But plastic articles will not decompose. Unless they are cleared up or buried, they will lie around forever and clutter the environment. In virtually every cove around England's coast, you will find plastic cups and bottles strewn along the high water mark.

The main problems with litter are that it is unsightly and that it wastes time and money to clear it away. Sometimes, it can be harmful. Broken bottles, old paint cans, discarded nylon fishing-line and lead shot can maim or poison wildlife. Rubbish dumped by the roadside can attract rats and become a health hazard.

People who drop litter and dump rubbish are either thoughtless or lazy. Litter bins are common in public places and every local council is required by law to provide a collection point where household rubbish can be dumped, free of charge. It is more difficult to understand people who are deliberately destructive. Unfortunately, broken lamps, walls scrawled over with graffiti and young trees snapped in half are common sights in some environments.

Urban areas suffer most, but rural areas, particularly farms, can also be the victims of mindless vandalism. Many farmers try to keep people off their land, because of the few stupid ones who damage crops, or, most distressing of all, injure farm animals.

Unless we can control both litter and vandalism, some of the aims of conservation will be impossible to achieve. What are the solutions? We can use warning notices and threats of fines (see the pictures on pages 16, 33, 34) but perhaps it would be better if people were encouraged to take an active part in conservation. One local authority had tried

It is a pity that the actions of a few people can spoil the environment for the majority. What can be done to stop it?

several times to plant some young trees on a local conservation project. Each time they were uprooted. Success was achieved only when the culprits were found and required to plant and care for the trees themselves. Why do you think this worked?

For conservation to succeed, responsibility has to be shared by everyone, and each person has to be aware of the consequences of his or her own behaviour. The problems of litter and vandalism make this point very well, because you can easily see the results of your own actions. How much litter is there in your playground or classroom? Make a collection of the litter around your school or neighbourhood. Write a report, saying where most of it was found (you could use a sketch map) and what the source and type of litter was — e.g., plastic, metal, paper, organic, etc. Produce a wall display or report on the effects of vandalism in your neighbourhood and indicate those areas which are most vulnerable.

Pollution

△

This is a typical busy traffic scene in a city centre. In what ways do you think it is adding to the pollution of the environment?

Pollution is caused when waste products from the enormous range of human activities accumulate in the environment in sufficient quantities to cause damage or unpleasantness. It is a problem which is as old as mankind, but which has forced itself on our attention more and more during the last few decades.

Most of us only become aware of pollution when it actually confronts our senses: for example, when we see smoke belching into the air from a chimney, or find our feet and clothes sticky with oil from a beach. However, there are numerous other kinds of pollution of which we are normally completely unaware because they are invisible — gases in the atmosphere caused by car exhausts for example, or the poisonous effects of some chemical wastes. In cases like these, pollution can be measured only by scientific experts using specialized methods and equipment.

Smoking chimneys used to be a major cause of air ▷ *pollution in city centres. The problem is much less severe now. How has this been achieved?*

Some kinds of pollution are more serious than others. The oil on the beach, for example, though an unpleasant nuisance, would eventually disperse, and its long-term effect on the environment would probably not be serious. On the other hand, the effect of car exhausts might become very serious indeed, because if the waste gases accumulate in the atmosphere to a sufficiently high concentration, they could cause a disastrous change in the world's climate by changing the effects of the sun's rays. Other kinds of pollution have a serious effect on wildlife and threaten the very existence of species of plants and animals.

If we want a pollution-free environment (or as near to this ideal as we can get), we shall

have to pay in order to achieve it. The pollution of rivers by sewage, for example, would be reduced if we paid for more sewage treatment works; and the pollution of the atmosphere would be less if we paid to have better exhaust systems fitted to cars. It is a question of priorities. Would you be prepared to pay more for the goods in the shops if that meant less pollution?

A great number of books have been written about the causes and effects of pollution, some of them at a simple level and others very advanced. If you want to find out more about this important topic, your local library will be able to help you to choose from this wide range. You can also find out whether there are any particular kinds of pollution which are having to be dealt with in your area. Pollution varies from region to region, depending on the kind of industries and other activities present. There might be stream pollution from agricultural fertilizers, perhaps, or air pollution caused by gases from a steel industry. Your local council should be able to help you here, and the regional office of the Department of the Environment, because it is part of their job to collect information about pollution. As for the wider situation, in Britain as a whole and throughout the world, you could begin a scrapbook of newspaper and magazine cuttings dealing with aspects of pollution, under the headings "air pollution", "pollution of the land" and "water pollution".

Recycling and Waste Avoidance

Every week the council dustcarts collect and dispose of millions of tons of rubbish. Houses, factories, offices, restaurants, places of entertainment — all those places where people live, work or gather together — have to be cleared of rubbish. The fact is that almost everything we eat, drink or use will end up sooner or later as waste. The food we eat becomes sewage; the wrapper around an ice-cream becomes waste paper within minutes of purchase; a new car may last for ten years or more, but it finishes as junk just the same. We cannot avoid things wearing out or becoming useless. As the population of the world increases and people in some countries get richer, so more and more goods of all kinds are consumed and more and more waste is produced.

This situation causes two problems. Firstly, there is the obvious need to dispose of all the waste products, and in densely populated places this is a major operation. Secondly, there is the need to keep on finding new resources of food and materials, to meet the ever-increasing demand for all the things we consume. Some resources are called "renewable resources", because they reproduce themselves naturally. These include all the products we get from plants and animals. Others are called "non-renewable resources" because, once they have been used up, they cannot be used again. The "non-renewables" include all the minerals we use, like coal, oil and all the metals.

If we are sensible and look after the "renewables" carefully, they will last forever, though some products could become scarce — like paper, for example, if we were to use up the trees more quickly than they can grow.

The "non-renewables" will eventually become scarce anyway, because the supplies of them are limited. After the year 2,000, for

example, it is likely that oil will be in short supply. It therefore makes sense to use all our resources sparingly. Our way of doing this is to separate waste into different materials and use some of them again. This is called ''recycling''.

We have been recycling some things for years. If you live in London, the water you get from your tap will already have been used several times, because some of London's water supply comes from treated sewage. Scrap metal dealers sort out the various metals from scrap for re-use. You can buy writing paper made from recycled waste paper. More and more councils are setting up collecting centres (bottle banks) where you can take used bottles for recycling into new glass.

Find out from your local council how it disposes of your rubbish and if any materials are sorted out for recycling. Find out if there is a bottle bank you can use, and what happens to the bottles. What do you think is the best kind of location for a bottle bank? Make a list of all the kinds of rubbish which are thrown away by your family in a week. Classify the various materials as ''renewables'' or ''non-renewables''. How much of this waste of materials could have been avoided (for example, by not using unnecessary packaging)?

Bottle banks like this are helping to popularise the idea of recycling resources. What is the purpose of the instructions on the container?

This is not an attractive part of conservation but this car-breaker makes a living from waste cars by selling spare engine parts and the crushed car bodies are recycled in the production of steel.
▽

Priorities

It is one of the unfortunate facts of life that there are more good causes than we could possibly find the resources or the energy to support. Every week seems to bring a different "flag day", with thousands of willing volunteers making street collections. All the causes are worthy, but we have to either share our donations among them all or choose to support some and not others. The decision is a problem for individual choice and priority.

The question of choice and priority arises in conservation too, because supporting conservation often means doing without something else. We have said that the extent to which pollution (pages 38-39) can be reduced will depend on our priorities, because, if more money is spent on clearing up pollution, then less is available for other kinds of spending. The money spent on a new sewage treatment plant might otherwise have been spent on a school or hospital. The choice is not easy. Some of the good causes competing for our support extend beyond the boundaries of our own country: for instance, the fight against famine and disease, relief for earthquake and flood victims, help for refugees. Every week brings more tragic news and a new request to which government and charity organizations try to respond. How high do you think conservation problems rank with these?

Britain is a wealthy country compared with most countries. Unlike people in the Third World, few British people lack the basic needs of food, clothing and shelter. We often criticize Third World countries for their lack of concern about conservation, but many in the Third World think that conservation is a luxury they cannot afford. They are too much concerned with the problem of keeping their families alive and well to worry about wildlife, landscape preservation, or smells. Do you think this is a reasonable viewpoint? Are there any aspects of conservation which should be of concern to the whole world?

What is more important, cheap electricity or unspoiled landscapes? Does the same answer apply for all areas?

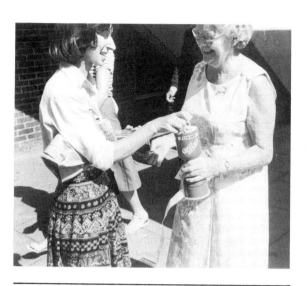

*Which of these good causes do you think should
receive the greatest priority, medical research,
concern for animals or problems of the Third World?
How can we make sure that we give attention to all
important causes?*

Find out what attitudes you and your
friends and family have towards conservation
matters, and what priority you give them.
Here is a list of topics which are linked in
some way with the conservation idea, arranged
in alphabetical order: archaeology, buildings
of historic interest, commons and footpaths,
conservation areas, landscape quality, litter,
museums, National Parks, noise, pollution
control, reclaiming derelict land, recycling
waste materials, trees and woodland, wildlife
and nature reserves. Try to regroup these
according to your own order of priorities.
Now make another list of important causes
— for example, medical research, education,
Oxfam, unemployment, and so on. Where
would you fit these into your list of priorities?
If you do this exercise with a group of your
friends, you will probably end up in an
interesting argument.

Lifestyles

A very interesting project is being carried out by a group of enthusiastic people near the town of Machynlleth in North Wales. There, based in an old slate quarry, you will find the National Centre for Alternative Technology. "Alternative technology" is a phrase used to describe a style of living which turns away from the "high technology" of the modern industrial countries, with their huge needs for energy and other resources, and prefers to use smaller, simpler and less wasteful methods.

The group in North Wales believe that it is possible to live a happy life without the great range of material comforts and possessions to which we have become accustomed, but without returning to the harsh conditions which many people had to endure before the modern era arrived with all its conveniences. They produce energy from the sun, wind and water, grow their own food on small, efficient plots of land, and produce very little waste or pollution. It is not a lifestyle which would suit everyone. Would you be happy without a family car, and using domestic sewage as a fertilizer for your vegetables? Nevertheless, it shows what can be done and provides a striking contrast with some aspects of modern society in wealthy nations like America and the countries of Western Europe.

According to some of the things we read in newspapers, or see and hear in some TV programmes and adverts, a better life is one in which we have more money to buy more of the exciting and attractive goods in the shops. It is true that not everybody in Britain is rich, but, as a country, we have come to expect,

What indications of growth and increasing consumption are there in this photograph? How do shops encourage us to keep buying more goods?

automatically, to have more and more with every passing year. Can you think of any ways in which this attitude could make the conservation of the environment more difficult? Remember, more goods require the use of more energy and more materials. Can you think of any ways in which your own lifestyle could be improved which would *not* require the use of more material resources?

More and more people are becoming convinced that we should be paying more attention to the conservation of the environment. The ideals of conservation are gaining support, and much progress has been made in the protection of the environment through laws and regulations. The increase in public interest

What do the signs in this photograph tell us about our lifestyles? Do they support the aims of conservation?

and concern about all conservation issues can be gauged from newspapers and magazines. You can make a study of this by checking through your national and local papers for, say, a month, and keeping a folder of cuttings on issues under discussion. At the end of the period, classify the items you have collected and write a summary to go with them, entitled "Conservation issues in (month, year)".

You can find out more about conservation by joining one of the conservation societies or organizations. Most libraries will have a list, with addresses, of national and local organizations concerned with all the topics raised in this book and more besides. Write to those that interest you and find out what their aims are and what activities they organize. You may find out that conservation is not just an ideal to aim for or to think about, but also a source of practical interest and enjoyment.

DIFFICULT WORDS

amenity the value or quality of being pleasant and attractive. An amenity landscape is one which has outstanding natural beauty or provides opportunity for leisure activities such as sightseeing and outdoor recreation.

biodegradable A biodegradable object is one which decomposes or rots through the activities of bacteria, fungi and such biological processes. In time, biodegradable materials "disappear", recycled and absorbed by the natural environment. Many manmade materials, especially plastics, are non-biodegradable and cannot be consumed in this way.

conservation and preservation These terms have similar but distinctive meanings when applied to the environment. "Preservation" is commonly used in the context of buildings and museum objects, and means that an item is kept or preserved in its original form. That is, there is no change. "Conservation", on the other hand, is generally applied to habitats, landscapes or raw materials which need management to ensure their continued existence. "Conservation" means the controlled use of things which are themselves growing or subject to change, like soil, forests or wildlife habitats and human landscapes.

decomposition the rotting or breaking up of materials into their constituent parts. When vegetation dies, it decomposes, to form humus, an important part of soil. Rocks also decompose; granite breaks down to produce "china clay" and residual grains of quartz.

derelict land According to the Department of the Environment, derelict land is "land so damaged by industrial or other developments that it is incapable of beneficial use without treatment". Many people think that the definition should be wider than this and should include all wasted or unused land.

deteriorate to grow worse or less useful.

environment the total surroundings which condition the growth or development of living things. Often it is helpful to think of the environment under headings, such as the urban or rural environment, or the natural or man-made environment.

extinct no longer existing.

fossil fuel a type of rock or natural deposit, like coal, petroleum or natural gas, which can be burnt to produce heat or energy. Fossil fuels are found within the earth's crust and were formed millions of years ago. Once used, they are gone forever; therefore they are known as non-renewable resources.

habitat the place where an organism lives. The habitat is an area where the requirements of a specific animal or plant are met in terms of climate, food, shelter, etc. Each species has its own ideal habitat in which it can best flourish.

heritage that part of culture which is handed down from the past, including landscapes, listed buildings, etc, as well as literature, music and other arts.

litter the rubbish, especially paper wrappings, tin cans, etc, dropped or thrown away in public places.

organic to do with living organisms like plants and animals and their remains.

pollution the introduction by man of waste materials and other products in sufficient quantities to cause damage to the environment.

preservation See Conservation.

pressure group a group of people seeking to use their influence in order to change or create policy for a particular purpose.

priority having a higher or an earlier place and rank in time or order of importance.

recreation the range of activities with which we fill our spare time, i.e. the time when we are not working. Many recreation activities have a direct effect upon the environment, e.g. the erosion of footpaths by walkers.

recycling reprocessing waste materials for re-use.

refurbishment the renovation and improvement of old property. Old houses can be refurbished by redecorating them and by adding modern facilities, like bathrooms.

sewage human and animal waste.

species a distinct group of plants or animals.

weathering and erosion Weathering is the breakdown of rock by chemical decomposition (i.e. chemical weathering) and by mechanical fragmentation (i.e. physical weathering, the splitting of rock by frost, etc) as a result of changes in temperature and moisture. Weathering produces a layer of rock waste which can then be removed by erosion. The agents of erosion are running water, ice, wind and waves.

PLACES TO VISIT

BOOK LIST

Wherever you live there will be a variety of places for you to visit, under the headings given below. To find out which are close to your local area, write to the organizations concerned or ask your local librarian for help.

(i) Museums

There are the national museums in London as well as city museums and smaller local institutions. The major open-air museums are:

North of England Open Air Museum, Beamish, Co. Durham.
Weald and Downland Museum, Singleton, Sussex.
Welsh Folk Museum, St. Fagan's, Cardiff.
Ulster Folk Museum, Co. Down.

(ii) National Parks, Areas of Outstanding Natural Beauty, Country Parks

Contact the Countryside Commission. (Addresses are on page 5.)

(iii) National Nature Reserves and Forest Parks

Contact the Nature Conservancy Council and the Forestry Commission.

(iv) Bird Reserves and Sanctuaries

Contact the Royal Society for the Protection of Birds.

(v) Historic Buildings and Amenity Areas

Contact the National Trust and the Civic Trust.

(vi) Conservation Areas and Town Trails

Contact the local authority.

(vii) Zoos

There are a number of zoos for you to visit. The principal ones are Regent's Park Zoo, London; Whipsnade Zoo, Bedfordshire; and at Edinburgh, Bristol, Chester, Dudley and Chessington.

(viii)   Visits can also be arranged to local parks, farms and to see how local authorities collect and dispose of waste.

Books marked with an asterisk (*) are most suitable for the teacher's use only.

*   Bentley, J.C. & Charlton, W.A., *Urban Dereliction* and *Gower: A Peninsula under Pressure* in "Resources and Environment Series" (slide-tape sets), Educational Productions Ltd, 1978

C.P.R.E., *Making a Tree Survey*, C.P.R.E.

*† D.E.S., *The Environment. Source of Information for Teachers. 1979,* H.M.S.O., 1979

King, A. and Conroy, C., *Paradise Lost?*, Friends of the Earth, 1980

Mabey, R., *The Common Ground*, Hutchinson

Mabey, R., *Pollution Handbook*, Penguin Books

*   Mills, D., *Geographical Work in Primary and Middle Schools*, Geographical Association, 1981

N.C.C., *Wildlife in the City*, Nature Conservancy Council, 1980

*   Ramblers' Association, *Public Footpaths : A Natural Teaching Resource*, R.A., 1981

Shoard, M., *Theft of the Countryside*, Temple-Smith, 1981

*   Town and Country Planning Association, *Bulletin for Environmental Education*, T.C.P.A.

*   Ward, B. & Dubos, R., *Only One Earth*, Pelican, 1972

Watch Society, *Your Garden as a Nature Reserve*, S.P.N.C.

Wilson, R., *The Backgarden Wildlife Sanctuary Book*, Astragal Books, 1980

Young, G., *Conservation Scene*, Peacock Books

Young, G., *Pollution*, Edward Arnold, 1980

*† Youth Environmental Action, *Up Your Street,* Y.E.A., 173, Archway Road, London, 1981

†These two publications provide excellent lists of organizations concerned with conservation, plus their addresses.

INDEX